TIME
FOR KIDS

Bad Guys and Gals
of the HIGH SEAS

Dona Herweck Rice

Consultants

Timothy Rasinski, Ph.D.
Kent State University

Lori Oczkus
Literacy Consultant

Marcus McArthur, Ph.D
Department of History
Saint Louis University

Based on writing from
TIME For Kids. *TIME For Kids* and the *TIME For Kids* logo are registered trademarks of TIME Inc. Used under license.

Publishing Credits

Dona Herweck Rice, *Editor-in-Chief*
Lee Aucoin, *Creative Director*
Jamey Acosta, *Senior Editor*
Lexa Hoang, *Designer*
Stephanie Reid, *Photo Editor*
Rachelle Cracchiolo, *M.S.Ed., Publisher*

Teacher Created Materials

5301 Oceanus Drive
Huntington Beach, CA 92649-1030
http://www.tcmpub.com
ISBN 978-1-4333-4902-7
© 2013 Teacher Created Materials, Inc.

Table of Contents

How to Spot a Pirate

You can easily recognize a pirate by the peg leg, eye patch, and parrot perched on his shoulder—right? If you're watching a movie, sure. Or reading a kid's book? You bet. But say you are standing on a Caribbean **dock** around 1700? Then, no, not so much.

A pirate was a sailor first. He wore clothes that any sailor would wear. The difference was that pirate gangs searched sea and shore to rob whatever they could find of value.

Today's Pirates

Pirates still exist today. They, rob, kill, and make people afraid. Today, pirates are most active off the coasts of Malaysia, Sumatra, Bangladesh, India, Brazil, and Somalia. Throughout the world, the cost of piracy (which includes both what is stolen and the cost to fight piracy) is as much as $12 billion per year!

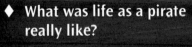

THINK LINK

- ◆ What was life as a pirate really like?

- ◆ Who were the fiercest pirates in the world?

- ◆ Why would someone want to become a pirate?

Risky Business

The pirates' goal was to raid ships or coastal towns. They took cash and gold, but also valuable goods, and even the ships themselves. This was risky business, but a pirate could make more money in a single **haul** than a sailor did in a lifetime.

Strangely, this goal did not belong to pirates alone. Sometimes, governments hired sailors as **privateers**. A privateer's job was to do exactly what pirates did. They took ships, gold, and goods from foreign ships during war. Privateers were licensed pirates.

A Pirate Without a Peg?

It's unlikely pirates long ago had peg legs or eye patches, because it would be difficult to survive as sailors in those times with only one leg or eye. And it's not likely that a parrot would want to sail out to sea to live the hard and dangerous life that a pirate lived.

James Madison, President of the United States of America,

TO ALL WHO SHALL SEE THESE PRESENTS, Greeting:

BE IT KNOWN, That in pursuance of an act of congress, passed on the *26th* day of *June* — one thousand eight hund̶ commissioned, and by these presents do commission, the private armed *Brig* called the *Abaellino* — of the burden of *On̶* s, or thereabouts, owned by *Henry Lewis & Winslow Lewis of Boston in the State of Massachus̶*

̶ting *Five* carriage guns, and navigated by *Seventy Six* ̶es *M. Fairfield* lieutenant of the said *Brig* men, hereby authorizing *William T. Wyer* ̶ed or unarmed British vessel, public or private, which shall be found within the jurisdictional limits of the United States, or elsewhere on t̶ and the other officers and crew thereof, to subdu̶ waters of the British dominions, and such captured vessel, with her apparel, guns, and appertenances, and the goods or effects which shall ̶, together with all the British persons and others who shall be found acting on board, to bring within some port of the United States; an̶ ̶l, goods, and effects of the people of the United States, which may have been captured by any British armed vessel, in order that proceedin̶ ̶ng such capture or recapture in due form of law, and as to right and justice shall appertain. The said *Wm. T. Wyer* is ̶n, seize, and take all vessels and effects, to whomsoever belonging, which shall be liable thereto according to the law of nations and the righ̶ power at war, and to bring the same within some port of the United States, in order that due proceedings may be had thereon. This comm̶ during the pleasure of the president of the United States for the time being.

States of America, at the City of Washington, the *̶ord, one thousand eight hundred and Fourteen̶*

The official papers that governments gave sailors to make them legal pirates, or privateers, were called *letters of marque*.

LETTER OF MARQUE
WAR OP 1812

Issued to Henry Lewis and Winslow Lewis of Boston
Dec.10, 1814 for the Brig Abaellino and signed by

The Jolly Roger

Pirate ships often hung a flag called the Jolly Roger. The flag was meant to warn other ships that the pirates would show no mercy and had no problem killing anyone who got in their way. The hope was that the attacked ship would give up easily, without a fight. The name Jolly Roger probably comes from the French words *joli rouge*, or "pretty red," which was likely the original color of the flag. Later, the flag was often black with a skull and crossbones—a warning of death.

A Pirate's Life

Judging by the movies, a pirate's life was once a leg-slapping, back-patting, rip-roaring, jolly good time! Who wouldn't want to cruise the high seas with Captain Jack Sparrow? Who wouldn't want to "pillage and **plunder**, rifle and loot" and "drink up, me 'earties, yo ho"? A pirate's life looks like a little mischief mixed with fun.

Truth or Fiction?

One of the most famous pirates known today is Captain Jack Sparrow. But he isn't a real figure from history. He is just a character played by Johnny Depp from the movie franchise *The Pirates of the Caribbean*.

actor Johnny Depp as Captain Jack Sparrow

The Golden Age of Piracy

Long ago, there was a period of time in which piracy was at an all-time high. No ship was safe on the water. Coastal towns were often at risk from pirate attacks. Different sources call different periods of time the Golden Age of Piracy. But the peak of this time seems to be about 1690 to 1730.

Blood, Sweat, and Tears

The truth is, the life of a pirate was hard and dangerous. During the Golden Age of Piracy, technology such as engines, radios, and GPS didn't exist. If it was cold at sea, pirates couldn't light a fire for warmth—a fire on board a wooden ship was dangerous! Pirates, like all sailors, had to keep their ships clean and well-maintained. Every sailor on board had to work constantly to care for the ship.

Cooking on Board

Sometimes, the crew needed to boil water or cook food. The cook would often heat bricks and cook with them. Or, a fire could be lit carefully during a calm sea. No sailor on a wooden ship was careless when it came to fire.

Pirates mainly chewed tobacco. Most avoided smoking on ships because it was a fire hazard.

Navigation

The **sextant** looks complex but the idea behind it is not. It measures the angle between an object in the sky and the **horizon**. Pirates and other sailors could then determine their location more accurately.

Pirates repaired any serious damage to their ships as quickly as possible.

Trust No One

Food had to be stored safely to stay dry for the long journey. If it went bad, then the crew didn't eat. If a dangerous storm brewed and the ship was thrashed about, they could only hope for safety. And if caught by the law, the punishment for piracy was death by hanging. That's if their intended **victims** didn't get them first!

Pirates may have had some successes along the way, but most of the time, they died young and poor. Many times, they fought among themselves or **mutinied** against their captain. After all, who can trust a pirate to follow the rules?

What in the world does me 'earties mean? It means "my hearties" or "my friends."

Rachel Wall

In the stories, most pirates are men. But in reality, women stormed the seas as well. Rachel Wall may have been the first American-born female pirate. She married a privateer at age 16, and after his death, lived a life of piracy, although she also worked as a servant. She was arrested after attempting to take a bonnet from another woman's head—and for trying to rip out the woman's tongue as well! Wall then asked to be tried as a pirate. She died at age 29, hanged for her crimes.

Pirates Welcome!

Believe it or not, there were several coastal towns that were known to welcome pirates. Pirates spent their money freely at the local saloons or on gambling. The towns may have figured if you can't beat 'em, join 'em!

DIG DEEPER!

SEA SHANTIES

Workers long ago were known to sing together while they worked to make their jobs a little easier. Pirates would have sung the same types of songs, or **sea shanties**, that most sailors did. Here are a couple shanties. There are different versions of these songs. Sing them if you know them!

Blow the Man Down

Come all ye young fellows that follow the sea.
Way, hey, blow the man down.
Now pay attention and listen to me.
Give me some time to blow the man down!

Oh, blow the man down, boys, blow the man down.
Way, hey, blow the man down.
Oh, blow the man down, boys, blow him away.
Give me some time to blow the man down!

As I was walking down Paradise Street,
Way, hey, blow the man down,
A pretty young damsel I chanced for to meet.
Give me some time to blow the man down!

Oh, blow the man down, boys, blow the man down.
Way, hey, blow the man down.
Oh, blow the man down, boys, blow him away.
Give me some time to blow the man down!

(The full song includes many verses.)

Cockles and Mussels

In Dublin's fair city, where girls are so pretty,
'Twas there that I met sweet Molly Malone.
She wheeled her wheelbarrow through streets broad
and narrow,

Crying, "Cockels and mussels alive, alive-o!
Alive, alive-o, alive, alive-o.
Crying, "Cockels and mussels alive, alive-o!"

She was a fishmonger, but sure 'twas no wonder,
For so were her father and mother before.
And they each wheeled their barrow through
streets broad and narrow,

Crying, "Cockels and mussels alive, alive-o!
Alive, alive-o, alive, alive-o.
Crying, "Cockels and mussels alive, alive-o!"

She died of a fever, and no one could
save her, And that was the end of
sweet Molly Malone. Her ghost wheels
her barrow through streets broad
and narrow,

Crying, "Cockels and mussels alive, alive-o!
Alive, alive-o, alive, alive-o.
Crying, "Cockels and mussels alive, alive-o!"

Captain Kidd

Captain William Kidd never wanted to be a pirate. In fact, he never thought he was one! But when he died, he was considered the most famous and cruelest pirate of his time.

Kidd was a family man with a wife and two grown daughters. As a **merchant**, he captained a ship about twice a year between his hometown of New York and London. He had once served in the British navy. Kidd followed the law, and he was a friend to the governor.

In 1695, a business partner made a proposition. He thought Kidd could captain a ship to catch pirates. Wealthy businessmen would **invest**. The investors and Kidd would share what was captured from the pirate ships. Kidd agreed, but then he had second thoughts. It might be risky and too hard to do. He decided to do it anyway.

Kidd had trouble from the start. He lost most of his first crew to the navy. He lost more to illness. The weather was bad, and they couldn't find any pirate ships.

Kidd's Commission

Kidd was **commissioned** to find pirate ships and bring back stolen goods. He was given letters that gave him the legal right to hunt pirates and also French ships, since France was England's enemy at that time. Even King William III gave Kidd a royal letter. The king would take 10 percent of the haul, although his name would never be mentioned.

Articles of Agreement,

Made the 10th Day of *October*, in the Year of our Lord 1695. Between the Right Honourable *RICHARD* Earl of *BELLOMONT* of the one part, and *Robert Levingston* Esq;

AND

Captain William Kid,

Of the other part.

WHEREAS the said Capt. *William Kid* is desirous of obtaining a Commission as Captain of a Private Man of War in order to take Prizes from the King's Enemies, and otherways to annoy them; and whereas certain Persons did some time since depart from *New-England*, *Rode-Island*, *New-York*, and other parts in *America* and elsewhere, with an Intention to become Pirates, and to commit Spoils and Depredations against the Laws of Nations, in the *Red-Sea* or elsewhere, and to return with such Goods and Riches as they should get, to certain places by them agreed upon; of which said Persons and Places, Capt. *Kid* hath notice, and is desirous to fight with and subdue the said Pirates, as also other Pirates with whom the said Capt. *Kid* shall meet at Sea, in case he be impowered so to do; and whereas it is agreed between the said Parties. That for the purpose aforesaid a good and sufficient Ship, to the likeing of the said Capt. *Kid* is to have the Com-...

Captain Kidd

Kidd is believed to have buried his treasure somewhere. This legend found its way into literature in Robert Louis Stevenson's *Treasure Island*.

Left Hanging

Kidd's tough crew grew restless. They wanted to capture pirate treasure! They didn't think Kidd was doing a good job. They decided to attack a ship and take its valuables.

The crew took over and turned the ship into a pirate vessel. Based on the crew's actions, Kidd got a reputation as a fierce pirate captain.

For three years, Kidd and his crew sailed the seas, "looking for pirates." When he made it back home, Kidd counted on his papers and friends to free him from piracy charges. They locked him up instead. After a year spent in a cold and damp jail cell, Kidd was tried and **convicted**. He wasn't allowed to speak at his trial. Kidd was hanged as a pirate.

Good Plan Gone Bad

Kidd wanted to be sure he could count on his crew. He chose family men who wanted to return to their wives and children back home. He also promised them a significant percentage of the haul. But the British Navy forced most of the crew to join the naval service. Kidd had to replace the crew with whomever he could find—sometimes pirates who were in between voyages. And he had to promise the new crew 60 percent of the haul!

Captain Kidd killed at least one mutinous pirate by throwing a bucket at his head.

Good and Dead

Kidd had to be hanged twice! The first time, the rope snapped. Then, his **executioners** hanged him again. His body was covered in tar and propped up in a metal cage. As his body rotted, the cage kept his skeleton upright. His bones were meant to warn everyone against a pirate's life.

X MARKS THE SPOT

In many pirate stories, pirates are forced to leave behind treasure and collect it when the coast is clear and times are safer. While this didn't happen often in real life, it probably happened sometimes. But after months at sea, it can be difficult to remember where you put something—even if that something is gold. Treasure maps were rumored to help pirates find where they hid their riches. The best maps used codes so the treasure wouldn't fall into the wrong hands.

Many old maps showed sea monsters in the water.

A harbor is a place where boats can float safely. Some harbors are natural. Some are man-made.

STOP! THINK...

- What dangers are shown on the map?

- Do you think this map gives enough detail to find the treasure many years after burying it?

- Why do you think the map shows an indirect route between the harbor and the treasure?

The letter *X* was often used to mark where the treasure was kept.

Pirates didn't use a standard measurement to note distances. A pace was the same distance as a step—as in, "Once at the beach, 500 paces ye must walk."

21

Blackbeard

Blackbeard the Pirate is one of the most remembered **buccaneers** from the Golden Age of Piracy. Born Edward Teach, his pirating name was inspired by his thick dark beard.

Blackbeard had a successful, but fairly short, career. He ruled in a unique way—with the permission of his crew. There are no reports of him killing or hurting his captives. His success came from two key factors. He had a sharp mind for pirate "business." He also used his frightening appearance to control his victims.

> Blackbeard's pirate career lasted only about two years, from 1716 until his death in 1718.

> Edward (Blackbeard) Teach, or perhaps Thatch, was born around 1680, probably in Bristol, England.

Blackbeard was famous for scaring enemies by tying fuses to his beard. The smoking hair let everyone know he meant business.

Stede Bonnet

Known as the Gentleman Pirate, Stede Bonnet was a wealthy landowner before he became a pirate. After being injured in a battle, Bonnet let Blackbeard captain his ship. When he was healed, the two pirates joined forces. Bonnet was captured but cleared of charges when he agreed to be a privateer against Spain. But he eventually returned to piracy—and suffered the fate of many pirates when he was captured, tried, and hanged.

23

Pirate Partners

Blackbeard's career began as a privateer during Queen Anne's War. He then joined Benjamin Hornigold's crew and became a true pirate. Hornigold quickly saw Blackbeard's skills, and he gave the pirate his own ship to command. When Hornigold retired, Blackbeard continued on his own. He set up an **alliance** of pirates who worked together to control the seas.

Queen Anne's War lasted from 1702 to 1713.

Queen Anne of England

Benjamin Hornigold

Hornigold helped Blackbeard in his career when he took on the young pirate as part of his crew. Hornigold saw Blackbeard's talents and gave him a position of **authority**. The captain enjoyed his best success when he worked with Blackbeard. But Hornigold finally gave up pirating and became a pirate hunter instead. Not for long, though. He was shipwrecked by a hurricane within a year.

The Blackbeard pirate alliance once held the entire town of Charleston, South Carolina for **ransom**.

Head Strong

Of course, Blackbeard made enemies. The governor of Virginia sent a small group of soldiers and sailors to capture the pirate. Unfortunately for Blackbeard, they were successful. Blackbeard was killed by a wound to the neck and many other stabbings. He was **decapitated**, and his head was hung from the **bowsprit** of his captor's boat.

Last Words

When Blackbeard was surrounded, he was quoted as exclaiming, "Damnation seize my soul if I give you quarters or take any from you." He meant that he had no intention of being captured or showing mercy to his attackers.

He Lost His Head

Blackbeard was killed by Lieutenant Robert Maynard and his crew. The pirate was singled out and surrounded, and he didn't stand a chance of getting out alive. Two slashes to his neck decapitated Blackbeard. Maynard kept the head in order to collect a reward.

Black Bart

John Bartholomew Roberts began his life at sea as a child—perhaps as young as age seven. He was a very experienced sailor. He even served his country in the navy. Roberts was an intelligent man and a hard worker. Everyone who sailed with him respected him. But he was also terribly cruel.

Black Bart didn't begin his pirating career until he was 37 years old.

Black Bart was born in Wales in 1682 and died in 1722 after three short, but successful, years of piracy.

Black Bart, born John Roberts, probably changed his name to Bartholomew Roberts in honor of the pirate Bartholomew Sharp—a pirate hero during Roberts's childhood.

Bartholomew Sharp

A successful pirate for three years, Sharp looted Spanish ships. Spain and England were not at war, so when Sharp was captured, Spain wanted him tried as a pirate. But Sharp had stolen a batch of useful Spanish maps, and the British king was grateful to have them. He cleared the pirate of all charges.

Black Bart

Aye, Aye Captain

Roberts had been sailing for about 30 years when pirates captured his ship. He and the other crew members were taken along. The pirates grew to admire Roberts. When their captain died, the pirates voted for a new captain. They voted for Roberts! Roberts knew he could make a lot of money. He also knew he could be a captain—something he didn't have a chance of becoming as a regular sailor. He accepted the post and became Black Bart.

Nowhere to Go

The highest rank Black Bart earned as a regular sailor was third mate. Third mate is fourth or fifth in command after the captain. The third mate is also in charge of safety. In Bart's time, it took having friends in high places to make a person a captain. Bart became a pirate mainly so he could have a chance to captain a ship.

Captured!

The Cervantes brothers of Spain were returning from war in 1575 when they were attacked and captured by pirates. They were sold into slavery in Africa. Their father was able to pay a ransom to free Roderigo, but his brother, Miguel, lived as a slave for five years before a ransom was accepted. Miguel Cervantes finally returned home and became a novelist—perhaps Spain's greatest writer and the author of the world-famous *Don Quixote*.

One reason for Black Bart's success may have been that—unlike so many other pirates—he rarely drank alcohol. His mind was always sharp. His favorite drink? Strong tea.

Reign of Terror

Black Bart's first act as a pirate was to go back to kill the people who had killed the pirate captain before him. He knew he must make others afraid of him to be successful. Once, Black Bart and his crew captured 22 ships, 150 fishing boats, and 40 cannons, even though the supplies were protected by 1,200 men. No one fought back. They were too afraid of Black Bart and his crew.

Goodbye, Black Bart

Bart was finally killed by a smattering of small bullets to his throat. To keep his body from capture, his loyal crew weighed it down with rocks and threw it overboard. It sunk to the depths of the ocean and was never found.

The King of Pirates

Henry Every, known as Long Ben, was a hero to England's poor. They saw him as a rebel who got the better of their wealthy rulers. During his pirate career from 1694 to 1696, Every stole millions of dollars. He escaped with his loot, and no one knows what became of him. Some say he became king of Madagascar. That is probably just a story, but people today still call him The King of Pirates.

Black Bart was killed during a battle at sea. His death marked the end of the Golden Age of Piracy.

Edward Low

As a young man, Edward Low of England moved to Boston in the American colonies. When his young wife died giving birth to their child, Low turned to pirating. He captained a small fleet of pirate ships.

Low was a fierce and cruel pirate. He burned most ships he captured and violently **tortured** his captives. He was savage, brutal, and showed no mercy.

Edward Low, originally called Ned, was born into poverty in 1690s England.

Low was born into a family of thieves and became a thief himself at a very young age.

Charles Vane

Charles Vane is not much remembered today, but he was well-known in his time. That was mainly because he was not only cruel to his captives but also disregarded the code of honor pirates used among themselves. He regularly cheated his crew out of their fair share. It's a wonder he was successful for as long as he was—about five years—which is a very long time in pirate years!

Walking the plank was a legendary way to kill a pirate.

A Deadly End

Low's pirating career lasted about three years, although its end is unclear. He may have been killed for murdering a fellow pirate or tried and executed by the French. He also may have been shipwrecked in a storm or even left to live out his life peacefully in Brazil.

The *New York Times* called Low "the most merciless pirate known to modern times" in 1892.

Charles Gibbs

Charles Gibbs

Charles Gibbs was an American pirate who pirated long after the Golden Age of Piracy. He was executed in 1831, one of the last people hanged for piracy in the United States. He told stories of his **exploits** while he was in prison. The stories became a very popular book after his death. The tales are highly detailed and seem exaggerated and extreme—so much so that many people doubt the truth of them.

Anne Bonny

Anne Bonny was raised as a girl and as a boy. Her father was an Irish lawyer and her mother was his housemaid. When the lawyer's wife found out, she had Anne's mother thrown in jail for theft. Her father took Anne into his house disguised as a boy and told everyone that Anne was his clerk.

Eventually, the lawyer's wife found out the truth, and there was a huge **scandal**. Anne and her parents took off for America to start a new life. Anne's father became a merchant and tried to find a wealthy husband for her, but Anne preferred the sailors she met on the docks. She married a pirate named John Bonny.

They aren't as well known, but women sailed as pirates, too.

Anne's mother died soon after the family arrived in America.

Whether they were male or female, pirates didn't limit themselves to one weapon. They often carried back ups.

Family Ties

John Bonny was a drunk, and Anne soon grew tired of him. Another handsome pirate began to flirt with her. Before long, Anne fell in love and ran away with the charmer whose name was Calico Jack.

Anne had a child with Jack, but she kept pirating with him, too. She also made a friend among his crew. The friend was another young woman named Mary Read, who also lived as a pirate.

No Women Allowed

The rule for most pirate ships was "no women allowed." In fact, a woman found on board a ship would probably be killed—along with anyone who helped her get there.

The fierce pirate Read fights another pirate.

Mary Read

Read, like Anne Bonny, was raised as a boy. As a young woman, Read joined the British Army, disguised as a man. After the war, she married as a woman. When her husband died, she turned to piracy to support herself. She was captured by Calico Jack and joined his crew. She and Anne Bonny worked side by side.

Captain John Rackham, Anne, and Read

Guilty

The two women suffered the same fate as the men when they were all captured and tried as pirates. First, the men were found guilty and hanged. Then, the women were convicted. But neither one was hanged for her crime because both were pregnant at the time. Read died in prison, but no one knows what became of Bonny. Some say her wealthy father was able to pay for her freedom and she died an old woman. But at the time of her trial she wasn't old at all. In fact, she was only about 20 years old.

Charlotte Badger

Probably the first female pirate from Australia, Charlotte Badger was a convict first. She went to prison in 1796 for stealing a small amount of money and a handkerchief to help support her very poor family. The pirate ship *Venus* was short on crew members so it took on convicts. The crew mutinied and took the ship from the captain, setting sail for New Zealand. It's not known what became of Badger.

Australia

New Zealand

"We Plead Our Bellies"

Anne and Read were both pregnant when convicted. They told the judge, "We plead our bellies." Their sentences were delayed until they gave birth. Read died of a fever in prison some time after giving birth. But there is no record of Anne's delivery, execution, death in prison, or release. It's a pirate mystery!

It's said that when she was captured, Anne's teeth were black and rotten. No one at the time had good dental care—especially pirates.

Lady Mary Killigrew

Mary Killigrew was married to a former pirate who was hired by Queen Elizabeth I to fight pirates. But when her husband, Sir John Killigrew, was away hunting, Lady Killigrew formed a pirate crew of her own. At that time in history, Queen Elizabeth I might have ignored piracy if it was done against the country's enemies. However, in 1570, Lady Killigrew's crew captured a ship that belonged to a friend of the queen, killing its crew and stealing the cargo.

Lady Killigrew lived in a castle in Cornwall, England.

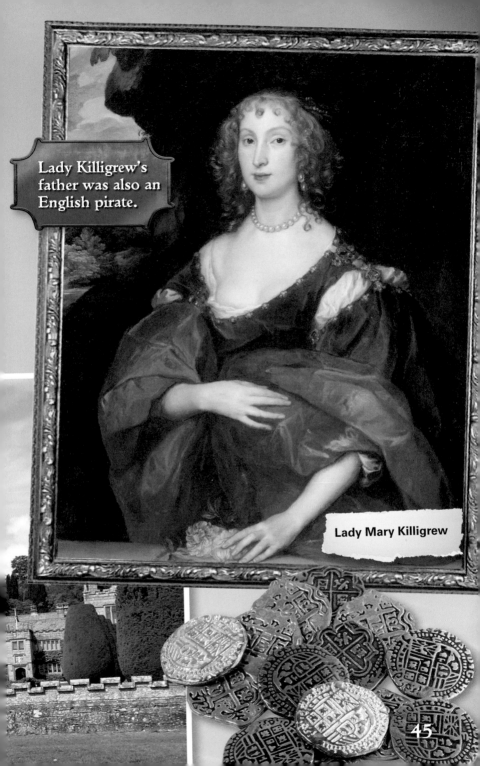

Lady Killigrew's father was also an English pirate.

Lady Mary Killigrew

Living by Her Own Rules

Queen Elizabeth wasn't happy and charged Killigrew with piracy, sentencing her to death. But the queen was forgiving, and Killigrew served just a short time in jail before being returned to her home.

Killigrew gave up pirating after that. Well, sort of. Rumors followed her for the rest of her years. She was said to **fence** stolen items for many years. Living within the law didn't seem to be her cup of tea.

It's possible Killigrew's family bribed the jury and she was let go. History isn't completely clear on that point—although it is clear that Killigrew did not hang for her crimes.

Queen Elizabeth I

Anne Dieu-le-Veut

Anne Dieu-le-Veut was a French pirate whose name meant "God wills it." She was given the name because it seemed as though everything came easily to her, or was given by God. When Dieu-le-Veut's husband was killed in a fight, she challenged his killer to a duel. He said he couldn't fight a woman. Instead he asked this fierce woman to marry him. Although they couldn't really marry (he was already married), they lived together as husband and wife. Dieu-le-Veut pirated side-by-side with her husband. But unlike Anne Bonny, this Anne lived her pirate life as a woman.

DIG DEEPER!

PIRATE SPEAK

"Damnation!" cried Blackbeard before heading to Davy Jones's locker. What does that mean? Take a look at these pages so you can talk like a pirate, too!

ahoy

ahoy—hello, but also goodbye

avast ye—stop and pay attention

bilge rat—the bilge is the bottom area of a ship, so a bilge rat is a creature that dwells there; a name to call one's enemy

black spot—a death threat from one pirate to another, made with a black mark on a paper given to the enemy

damnation—used to emphasize frustration or anger

Davy Jones's locker—an imaginary spot at the bottom of the ocean where pirates go when they die

grog—a mix of water and rum, with the rum being added to disguise the taste of water gone bad

landlubber—a slow and clumsy person who is not very agile or surefooted on a ship

bilge rat

48

grog

quarter—although officially meaning "shelter," pirates used *quarter* to mean mercy

salmagundi—a popular pirate meal made of chopped meat, eggs, onions, grapes, cabbage, seasonings, and more, all mixed together

shiver me timbers—an expression of disbelief, probably coming from the shock to the wooden timbers of a ship when it runs aground

landlubber

to go on account—to become a pirate, or the pirate version of going into business

walk the plank—the pirate practice of making a victim walk off the side of a ship into the ocean below and therefore to his or her death by drowning; although commonly seen in movies, it may have never actually happened

walk the plank

Mrs. Cheng

A tiny woman ruled a fleet of more than 500 pirate ships in the seas around China. She was known simply as Mrs. Cheng. Mrs. Cheng's husband had once been the admiral of this pirate fleet. But he was killed and she took over, making the fleet even more powerful. It became too big and strong for the Chinese government to fight. The people just had to hope for the best!

Cheung Po Tsai

With a name that means Cheung Po the Kid, Cheung was kidnapped by Mrs. Cheng and her husband when he was just 15. They adopted the boy, and he took over part of their empire. When the Cheng pirate dynasty ended, Cheung became a navy colonel for the Chinese government and lived the rest of his life in the service.

Mrs. Cheng, born in about 1775, pirated until 1810 and lived peacefully until dying naturally in 1844.

Never Surrender

The government finally succeeded when one of Mrs. Cheng's leaders gave himself up in exchange for a pardon and two islands on which his family and crew could live. Weakened, Mrs. Cheng finally also accepted a pardon and a large sum of money. She gave up her life of piracy—only to run a successful **smuggling** empire the rest of her life!

A Pirate Army

In its heyday, Chinese piracy was far more powerful than Caribbean piracy. At one point, there were about 50,000 Chinese pirates. Even during the *Golden Age of Piracy*, there were never more than 6,000 pirates in the Caribbean.

Before battle, Mrs. Cheng's pirates drank a mixture of gunpowder and alcohol. It made their eyes red, which in turn frightened their captives.

Sir Henry Morgan

Sir Henry Morgan is most noted for his amazing luck as a pirate. In 1669, his pirate ship exploded, but he was thrown through a **porthole** and lived. In 1675, his ship was wrecked in a hurricane, but Morgan again survived. And despite all his exploits as a pirate, the government let him do it as a privateer. In fact, he was named Sir Henry and given a **plantation** in Jamaica, where he lived very well until he was 53. Then he died of alcohol poisoning from all the pirate rum he drank!

A Motley Crew

For years, pirate crews of old sailed the seas, plundering, looting, and taking what they could. As feared as they were, many people saw them as heroes. People wanted to hear about their adventures, and children dreamed of joining the fun. Even today, people flock to movies about pirate exploits. We know that pirates stole, terrorized, and killed, so what makes us long to hear their stories? Are the stories so terrible that we can only believe they are fiction—made up to thrill our imaginations?

The stories are only too real, as pirate survivors know. And as they say in pirate lore, "Dead men tell no tales."

Pirates in battle had to be prepared to make the first move or risk being killed.

Governments sometimes displayed pirate heads in wooden boxes as a reminder of the dangers of pirating.

A pirate's life was filled with violence and hardship.

SURVIVORS

Some people lived to tell the tale of what they experienced at the hands of pirates. Here are a few of the most famous stories—and proof that pirate stories are true stories, indeed.

Quakers

Quakers are religious people who do not believe in war or violence. So when a crew of Quakers was captured by pirates, they did not fight back. They had no weapons, and they would not have used them anyway. The pirates were at ease with this peaceful bunch. They went below deck to sleep. While there, the Quakers removed the pirates' weapons and locked the pirates below deck. They then delivered the pirates home before making their own way back to England.

George Fox, English founder of the Society of Friends, or Quakers

Father Vincent de Paul

French priest Father Vincent de Paul was on a ship in 1605 when it was captured by pirates. The brutal crew killed many, even hacking one sailor into a thousand pieces. He lived, but was sold into slavery with other survivors. For several years he lived as a slave, far from home. He finally escaped, and walked many miles back to France. His experiences made him determined to help others who suffered. Father Vincent de Paul helped to free about 1,500 slaves, and 77 years after his death he was named a **saint**.

Captain Snelgrave

Captain William Snelgrave and his crew were captives of a pirate crew for a month before they were released. When Snelgrave's crew begged for his life, the pirates let him live. It meant a great deal to the pirates to see a captain so respected by his crew. The pirates argued as to whether they should let the crew live. They finally decided to let them go and gave them a ship and treasure worth several thousand English pounds. After several weeks, the crew finally made it home to tell their amazing story.

Glossary

alliance—a partnership made for mutual support and protection

authority—leadership

bowsprit—the long pole that juts out from the front of a ship

buccaneers—privateers

commissioned—hired, especially by a government or its agent

convicted—sentenced as guilty of a crime

decapitated—cut off the head of a person or animal

dock—a structure that sticks out into a body of water from the mainland so that boats can be tied up to it and parked, or docked

executioners—people responsible for killing those who are sentenced to death

exploits—adventures

fence—to accept and sell stolen goods

haul—treasure or riches gathered

horizon—the line where the earth or sea appears to meet the sky

invest—to pay money to support a business or cause, with the purpose of making more money

merchant—a salesperson, especially one who runs a store

mutinied—overthrew a ship's authority to take leadership, usually by killing or otherwise getting rid of the captain

plantation—a large agricultural estate worked by laborers

plunder—to rob goods or valuables by force

porthole—a window with a cover in the side of a ship

privateers—pirates commissioned by a government to capture and loot enemy ships

ransom—a payment made to free a person or thing from those who have taken it illegally

saint—a highly holy person honored in some religious faiths

scandal—a story that brings shame to the people in it

sea shanties—songs sung by sailors and pirates

sextant—an instrument for measuring distances, often used for navigation

smuggling—illegally moving goods from one place to another

tortured—harmed through physical and mental pain

victims—people cheated, injured, or killed by another

Index

Bibliography

Beahm, George. *Caribbean Pirates: A Treasure Chest of Fact, Fiction, and Folklore.* **Hampton Roads Publishing Company, Incorporated, 2007.**

Discover the answers to all of your pirate questions, including whether cursed Aztec gold really existed. You'll also find suggestions for tons of cool pirate books, museums, festivals, movies, and websites to check out.

Hecker, Alan and Alisha Niehaus. *Piratepedia.* **DK Publishing, 2006.**

Get your sea legs ready for a swashbuckling adventure! Sail back in time, and meet pirates, corsairs, and buccaneers on the high seas around the world. You'll learn how to avoid slavery, survive a pirate attack, and fend off starvation while stranded at sea.

Seidman, David and Jeff Hemmel. *The Anti-Pirate Potato Cannon: And 101 Other Things for Young Mariners to Build, Try & Do on the Water.* **McGraw-Hill, 2010.**

The activities, projects, and facts in this guide about boating, sailing, and the sea will turn you into an expert mariner in no time. Build an anti-pirate potato cannon, tie knots like a nautical pro, navigate by the stars, and more!

Yolen, Jane. *Sea Queens: Women Pirates Around the World.* **Charlesbridge Publishing Incorporated, 2010.**

Follow the adventures of bold women in history who defied society's rules and pirate laws by becoming raiders on the high seas. Some of these daring dames were even more notorious than their male counterparts.

More to Explore

Disney Pirates of the Caribbean
http://disney.go.com/pirates

Learn all about the story and characters of *Pirates of the Caribbean: On Stranger Tides*. Watch videos and see photos from the film, captain your own pirate ship, or craft a Jack Sparrow doll.

Kaboose: Pirates
http://funschool.kaboose.com/time-warp/pirates/

Avast, me hearty! Prepare to pillage, plunder, and have a jolly good time with these free online games. Help Puke the Pirate collect Black Barf's treasure or protect a pirate's loot from sharks. Then, keep your pirate skills sharp with puzzles, crafts, and coloring pages.

National Geographic Pirates
http://www.nationalgeographic.com/pirates/

Experience Pirate Terror at Sea with Blackbeard in the Caribbean. Explore North America's only pirate shipwreck and meet its captain, Sam Bellamy, and his crew. Then, test your pirate IQ by solving three high seas adventures.

Pirate Ship of Fools
http://www.kidsgamehouse.com/games/pirate-ship-of-fools/

Join Scooby-Doo and Shaggy on a terrifying Horror on the High Seas adventure. Help these fainthearted sleuths solve the mystery of the Ghost Pirate. Your challenge is to find clues, pick up items that help you overcome obstacles, and keep the skittish duo's "Fear-o-Meter" down.

About the Author

Dona Herweck Rice grew up in Anaheim, California, and graduated from the University of Southern California with a degree in English and from the University of California at Berkeley with a credential for teaching. She has been a teacher in preschool through tenth grade, a researcher, a librarian, and a theater director. She even worked on the Pirates of the Caribbean ride at Disneyland. She is now an editor, a poet, a writer of teacher materials, and a writer of books for children. She is married with two sons and lives in Southern California.